The
diabetes

HEALTH FOR LIFE

Everyday Cookbook

JODY VASSALLO

with Susanna Holt, Ph.D.

MARLOWE & COMPANY
New York

ABOUT DIABETES

On average, almost ten percent of the population in western countries have diabetes and unfortunately this number continues to rise. But there are steps anyone can take to either reduce the risk of developing the disease; control the disease once it is diagnosed; or possibly even reverse the condition. In the past, diets for diabetics were relatively limited and often stressful. Thanks to scientific research, it is now known that a diabetic diet does not have to be so stringent, and moderate amounts of sweet foods can usually be included. A low-fat diet based on low-GI, carbohydrate-rich foods is an important part of the recommended therapy for people with diabetes. This book provides diabetics with general guidelines for healthy eating and contains delicious recipes to assist in achieving these goals. The recipes are also nutritionally analyzed and GI-rated. However, the information in this book should not replace any advice given to you by a doctor or dietitian. Your individual health needs may require specific dietary restrictions or changes, so check with both your doctor and dietitian before making any changes to your diet, exercise habits or medication to make sure that they are safe for you.

Dr. Susanna Holt
(Ph.D. and registered dietitian)

WHAT IS DIABETES?

Diabetes is a condition in which the blood sugar (glucose) level is excessively high for one of two reasons: either the body cannot produce enough insulin, or the body cannot use insulin properly. In both healthy people and diabetics, blood sugar rises after eating as the food's carbohydrates are digested into glucose and absorbed into the blood. In healthy people, the rise in blood sugar stimulates the pancreas to release a hormone called insulin. Insulin enables body cells to absorb the glucose and fats in the blood, causing the blood sugar level to fall back down to normal. In people with diabetes, the pancreas doesn't make enough insulin or the cells don't respond to it properly, so glucose and fats cannot get into the body's cells and build up in the blood. The blood sugar rises to a higher level after eating, doesn't fall as quickly and remains higher than normal, even many hours after eating. If left untreated, the high blood glucose and fat levels can damage the eyes, nerves and blood vessels and increase the risk of heart disease, kidney and circulatory problems. Symptoms of undiagnosed diabetes can include frequent urination, excessive thirst, tiredness, infections and leg cramps. Early diagnosis and appropriate treatment are an essential part of minimizing the risk of the serious health problems associated with diabetes.

TYPES OF DIABETES

There are three main types of diabetes and a pre-diabetic condition:

1 | **Type 1 (insulin-dependent or juvenile-onset diabetes)** - is the most serious but least common form and mostly occurs in normal weight children and young adults. People with type 1 diabetes cannot make the hormone insulin due to a damaged pancreas and require daily insulin injections to stay alive.

2 | **Type 2 (non-insulin dependent or adult-onset diabetes)** - is the most common form and usually develops in overweight people after the age of 40 due to the body not responding to insulin properly. The risk of developing type 2 diabetes is increased by being overweight and inactive, having a family history of diabetes, and eating too much fat and refined carbohydrates. Treatment revolves around healthy eating, weight control and physical activity.

3 | **Gestational** - is a temporary form of diabetes that develops in some women during pregnancy because certain hormones stop insulin from working properly. It usually disappears once the pregnancy is over, but if left untreated can result in a difficult delivery and health problems in the infant. It is usually detected during a routine blood test at 24–28 weeks, and is generally treated with healthy eating alone. Gestational diabetes increases the risk of developing type 2 diabetes later in life, but this can be reduced with a healthy lifestyle.

Impaired glucose tolerance (IGT) - is a pre-diabetic condition where blood glucose is higher than normal but not in the diabetic range. IGT increases the risk of developing type 2 diabetes but this can be prevented with a healthy diet and regular exercise, both of which are more effective than medication. As little as 30 minutes a day of moderate physical activity, such as brisk walking, coupled with some weight loss, will improve your health.

MANAGING DIABETES

The main goal is to keep blood glucose within a relatively normal range to prevent problems such as heart disease, kidney failure and blindness. Diabetes is a long-term problem, so you will need to make lifestyle changes and learn to monitor your condition by:

1 | eating a healthy diet and maintaining a healthy weight
2 | getting regular physical activity and reducing stress levels
3 | taking any diabetes-related medication prescribed for you
4 | not smoking and only drinking alcohol in moderation, if at all
5 | regularly checking your blood sugar
6 | consulting your doctor and other relevant health professionals.

STEPS TO HEALTHY EATING

1 | Eat low-GI, carbohydrate-rich meals

Eating 4–6 smaller carbohydrate-rich meals and snacks, spread over the day, rather than 2–3 large meals will help control blood glucose. Ask your dietitian for advice about scheduling food intake around medication and activity patterns. Monitoring your blood glucose will also help you find out when and what you should eat, or if you've eaten too much.

2 | Limit total fat (particularly saturated fat)

Eating too much saturated fat can cause weight gain, poor blood glucose control and high blood cholesterol, all of which are known to increase the risk of heart disease. Try to use low-fat cooking methods and choose low-fat dairy products, lean meat and poultry, and low-fat spreads. Limit your intake of fried and fast foods, cookies, pastries and cakes. Use small amounts of canola or olive oil when cooking and eat oily fish 2–3 times each week to make sure you get enough healthy essential omega-3 fats.

3 | Increase fruit and vegetable intake

Aim to eat at least 2 servings of fruit and 5 servings of vegetables each day. They will help you feel full, and in addition they contain many healthy nutrients, including antioxidants that can help protect tissues from being damaged by excess blood glucose.

4 | Limit sugar and sugary food intake

Sugar doesn't cause diabetes and people with well-controlled diabetes don't have to avoid sugar completely but it should be treated with caution, especially if you need to lose weight. Adding a little sugar (or, better still, fresh fruit) to a bowl of porridge or bran cereal won't raise blood sugar very much, but having a soft drink or lollies in between meals will send it soaring. Reduced-sugar products are readily available and provide sweetness without too many calories or raising blood sugar.

5 | Limit salt intake

Excess salt raises blood pressure, which increases the risk of heart and kidney disease. Avoid adding salt to meals and look for reduced- or no-added salt versions of canned and packaged foods. Use herbs, spices, lemon juice and vinegar for flavor.

6 | Limit alcohol intake

Alcohol is high in calories so avoid it if you are trying to lose weight or have poorly controlled diabetes. Health authorities recommend drinking a maximum of 1–2 standard drinks a day, with alcohol-free days each week. Choosing low-alcohol beer or diluting wine and spirits with soda water or a diet soft drink are better choices. If you take diabetic medication, you must eat some carbohydrate (such as bread or low-fat crackers) whenever you drink alcohol to reduce the risk of hypoglycemia.

THE GI GUIDE

low-fat custard gi 37

boiled dried legumes gi 18-46

dried temperate fruit gi 30

low-fat milks gi 30

carrots gi 41

berries gi 40

raw rolled oats gi 58

apples gi 38

citrus gi 25-42

natural muesli gi 39-66

high-amylose rice gi 48-58

garden peas gi 48

Not all carbohydrates cause a blood sugar spike. In fact, the amount of sugar or starch in a food is not a good indication of its blood glucose (glycemic) effect. There are many different types of sugars and starches, and they are digested at different rates and have different effects on blood glucose. Preparation and cooking methods will also affect the blood glucose response. The more processed a food is, the easier it is to digest and the higher its glycemic index (GI) value. Scientists developed the GI method to measure the extent to which different carbohydrate-rich foods increase blood glucose when eaten.

le-grain breads gi 38-55

noodles gi 26-62

pears gi 38

pearl barley gi 25

nned legumes gi 14-56

low-fat ice cream gi 37-47

bulghur gi 48

durum wheat pasta gi 27-61

semolina gi 54

orange sweet potato gi 54

sweet corn gi 54

low-fat yogurt gi 20-33

Although they contain the same amounts of carbohydrate, foods with a high GI value (>70) are digested faster and produce a quicker and higher rise in blood glucose than foods with a medium (56–69) or low GI value (<55). People with diabetes should choose carbohydrate-rich foods with low to medium GI values. Switching from high- to low-GI foods, limiting fat intake and exercising regularly will improve your health. At the end of every recipe in this book is a list of the nutrients contained in each serving of the dish, as well as its estimated GI value. For more GI information see www.glycemicindex.com

BREAKFAST

layered berry shake

LAYERED BERRY SHAKE

1²/₃ cups fresh or frozen
   raspberries

1¹/₃ cups sliced strawberries

1 medium-size ripe banana

2 tablespoons oat bran

1 Weet-Bix or other similar
   breakfast cereal

1 tablespoon honey

2 tablespoons non-fat, sugar-free
   vanilla yogurt

2 cups skim or non-fat milk

1 Put the raspberries into a blender and blend until smooth. Divide the puree among 4 glasses.

2 Put the remaining ingredients into the blender and blend until thick and creamy.

3 Carefully pour over the raspberry puree to form 2 separate layers. Serves 4

per serving | fat 1 g | protein 9.5 g | carbohydrate 28 g | fiber 5.5 g | cholesterol 6 mg | energy 175 cal | gi 41 ▼ low

OATMEAL WITH CARAMELIZED APPLES

1 cup raw rolled oats

¹/₄ cup semolina

2 tablespoons unprocessed
   oat bran

1 teaspoon vanilla

3 cups water

2 teaspoons reduced-fat
   polyunsaturated margarine

2 medium-size red apples,
   unpeeled and cut into rounds

¹/₂ teaspoon ground cinnamon

¹/₂ cup unsweetened apple juice

1 cup reduced-fat milk

1 Put the rolled oats, semolina, oat bran, vanilla and water into a pan and cook over medium heat for 5−10 minutes, stirring occasionally until the oatmeal is thick and creamy.

2 Heat the margarine in a non-stick frying pan, add the apples and cinnamon and cook over medium heat until the apples are browned on both sides.

3 Add the apple juice and cook over high heat until the liquid has evaporated and the apples are soft.

4 Spoon the oatmeal into bowls, top with the milk and finish with the caramelized apples. Serves 4

per serving | fat 4 g | protein 7 g | carbohydrate 40 g | fiber 4.5 g | cholesterol 2 mg | energy 225 cal | gi 43 ▼ low

oatmeal with caramelized apples

french toast with berries & yogurt

FRENCH TOAST WITH BERRIES & YOGURT

1 Whisk together the eggs, milk and sugar or sweetener and dip the bread, one slice at a time, into the egg mixture.

2 Heat a non-stick frying pan over medium heat and cook the bread until the egg has set and the bread is golden brown on both sides. Keep the finished slices warm while the remaining slices are cooked.

3 Serve stacks of the bread topped with yogurt and berries. Serves 4

per serving (sugar) | fat 5.2 g | protein 20 g | carbohydrate 53.8 g | fiber 5.6 g | cholesterol 104 mg | energy 355 cal | gi 37 ▼ low

per serving (sweetener) | fat 5.2 g | protein 20 g | carbohydrate 46.4 g | fiber 5.6 g | cholesterol 104 mg | energy 327 cal | gi 32 ▼ low

2 eggs, lightly beaten

1 cup skim or non-fat milk

2 tablespoons sugar or low-calorie sweetener suitable for cooking

8 slices whole-grain bread

1²/₃ cups non-fat, sugar-free vanilla yogurt

2 cups mixed fresh or frozen berries

corn, eggs & smoked salmon toast

CORN, EGGS & SMOKED SALMON TOAST

1 Cut the bread into 4 x 1-inch thick slices, toast and spread it with margarine.

2 Whisk the eggs and milk together and cook in a non-stick frying pan over medium heat. Stir until the eggs just begin to scramble, then stir in the creamed corn.

3 Cook for 3 minutes or until heated through. Season with cracked black pepper. Serve the toast topped with the corn mixture and smoked salmon. Serve the spinach to the side. Serves 4

per serving | fat 10.5 g | protein 24 g | carbohydrate 52.5 g | fiber 7.5 g | cholesterol 201 mg | energy 400 cal | gi 48 ▼ low

1 small loaf whole-grain bread

2 teaspoons reduced-fat polyunsaturated margarine

4 eggs, lightly beaten

3/4 cup skim or non-fat milk

1 1/4 cups creamed corn

cracked black pepper

3 1/3 oz smoked salmon

2 cups baby spinach

SPICED COUSCOUS, FRUIT COMPOTE & YOGURT

1 Put the couscous, dried fruit, cranberries and pistachio nuts into a bowl.

2 Heat the milk, cinnamon and cardamom in a pan and bring just to the boil. Pour the milk over the couscous and allow to stand for 10 minutes or until the liquid has been absorbed.

3 Remove the cinnamon and cardamom and serve bowls of couscous, topped with yogurt. Serves 6

per serving | fat 3.1 g | protein 11.1 g | carbohydrate 72.9 g | fiber 5.3 g | cholesterol 5 mg | energy 368 cal | gi 47 ▼ low

1 cup couscous

1 2/3 cups assorted roughly chopped dried fruit (apple, pear, peach, apricot)

1/2 cup firmly packed dried cranberries

1/4 cup pistachio nuts, roughly chopped

2 cups skim or non-fat milk

1 cinnamon stick

4 cardamom pods, bruised

3/4 cup non-fat, sugar-free vanilla yogurt

spiced couscous, fruit compote & yogurt

cheesy baked bean omelette

CHEESY BAKED BEAN OMELETTE

4 eggs, lightly beaten

2 tablespoons chopped
   fresh parsley

1 tablespoon reduced-fat
   polyunsaturated margarine

6¹/₂ oz can reduced-salt
   baked beans

¹/₃ cup grated reduced-fat
   cheddar cheese

1 Whisk the eggs and parsley together.

2 Melt the margarine in a 12-inch non-stick frying pan. Pour in the egg mixture and swirl to coat the base of the pan.

3 Cook over medium heat for 3 minutes until the sides begin to set, then gently lift the edge and allow the uncooked egg to run underneath.

4 Top with baked beans, evenly spread, and sprinkle with the grated cheese. Cook for 3 minutes or until the underneath just begins to set. Fold in half using an egg slice. Cut into wedges and serve with toasted whole-grain bread. Serves 4

per seving | **fat 9 g** | **protein 12 g** | **carbohydrate 6 g** | **fiber 2.5 g** | **cholesterol 193.5 mg** | **energy 150 cal** | **gi 46** ▼ **low**

WARM FRUIT SALAD WITH YOGURT

1 lb 6¹/₂ oz peeled cantaloupe,
   sliced

1¹/₃ cups strawberries,
   cut into halves

2 medium-size kiwifruit, peeled
   and sliced

3 cups chopped pineapple

¹/₃ cup passionfruit pulp or
   orange juice

¹/₂ cup unsweetened pineapple
   juice

³/₄ cup low-fat plain yogurt

1 cup natural muesli

1 Put the cantaloupe, strawberries, kiwifruit and pineapple into a bowl and gently mix to combine.

2 Put the passionfruit or orange juice and pineapple juice into a pan, gently heat until warm and stir to combine.

3 Pour over the fruit salad and gently mix to coat the fruit in the liquid.

4 Spoon fruit salad into wide-topped glasses and top with a spoonful of yogurt and muesli. Serves 4

per seving | **fat 3.6 g** | **protein 10.6 g** | **carbohydrate 48.8 g** | **fiber 12.4 g** | **cholesterol 2.3 mg** | **energy 299 cal** | **gi 54** ▼ **low**

warm fruit salad with yogurt

SWEET POTATO CAKES WITH ARUGULA SALAD

3^1/$_2$ cups peeled, grated orange
   sweet potato
1 egg, lightly beaten
1 tablespoon all-purpose flour
olive oil spray
4 medium-size vine-ripened
   tomatoes, halved lengthwise
cracked black pepper
1 cup baby arugula
1 small avocado, peeled and cut
   into wedges

1 Preheat oven to 400°F.

2 Squeeze out any excess moisture from the sweet potato and discard it.

3 Add the egg and flour to the sweet potato and mix gently to combine.

4 Shape 2 tablespoons of the mixture into 8 balls and flatten slightly to make evenly sized potato cakes. Arrange on a non-stick baking tray, spray lightly with olive oil spray, and bake for 25–30 minutes or until cooked through.

5 Put the tomatoes onto a non-stick baking tray, sprinkle with cracked black pepper and bake at the same time as the potato cakes for 30 minutes or until they are soft.

6 Divide potato cakes among 4 plates and serve with tomatoes, arugula and avocado. Serves 4

per serving | fat 13.5 g | protein 7 g | carbohydrate 21 g | fiber 3 g | cholesterol 47 mg | energy 235 cal | gi 52 ▼ low

sweet potato cakes with arugula salad

crunchy apple-filled muffins

CRUNCHY APPLE-FILLED MUFFINS

1 Preheat oven to 375°F. Lightly spray a 6 x ½ cup capacity non-stick muffin pan with canola oil spray.
2 Sift the flours and cinnamon into a bowl, stir in the brown sugar or sweetener, and make a well in the center. Whisk together the egg, buttermilk and oil, pour into the well and fold in gently until just combined.
3 Half-fill each muffin hole using half the total mixture, top with a spoonful of apple pie filling, then fill each muffin hole with the remaining mixture.
4 Sprinkle the combined rolled oats and extra sugar over the top and bake for 20 minutes, or until the muffins are risen and start to come away from the side of the pan. Allow to cool for a couple of minutes before turning out on a wire rack to cool. Makes 6

per muffin (sugar) | fat 9 g | protein 8 g | carbohydrate 47 g | fiber 4.5 g | cholesterol 35 mg | energy 295 cal | gi 62 ◆ med

per muffin (sweetener) | fat 9 g | protein 8 g | carbohydrate 38 g | fiber 4.5 g | cholesterol 35 mg | energy 265 cal | gi 60 ◆ med

* To convert all-purpose flour to self-rising flour, add 2 level teaspoons of baking powder to 1 cup of all-purpose flour.

canola oil spray
1 cup whole-wheat self-rising flour*
1 cup self-rising flour*
1 teaspoon ground cinnamon
¼ cup brown sugar or low-calorie
   sweetener suitable for cooking
1 egg, lightly beaten
1 cup buttermilk
2 tablespoons vegetable oil
6½ oz can apple pie filling
2 tablespoons raw rolled oats
1 tablespoon brown sugar, extra

PHYLLO FRUIT & NUT SHEETS WITH SPICED MILK

4 sheets phyllo pastry
³/₄ cup golden raisins
¹/₂ cup walnuts, roughly chopped
¹/₄ cup flaked almonds
4 cups skim or non-fat milk
¹/₂ teaspoon ground cinnamon

1 Preheat oven to 400°F.

2 Lay the phyllo sheets out flat in single layers on 2 non-stick baking trays. Bake for about 15 minutes or until crisp and golden. Break the sheets into large pieces.

3 Arrange a layer of cooked phyllo in 4 individual cereal bowls, top with some golden raisins, walnuts and almonds, top with more pastry and finish with the remaining golden raisins and nuts.

4 Heat the milk and cinnamon in a pan just until it comes to the boil. Pour the hot milk over the layered fruit and phyllo and serve immediately. Serves 4

per serving | fat 13.5 g | protein 14.5 g | carbohydrate 40.5 g | fiber 3 g | cholesterol 18 mg | energy 335 cal | gi 48 ▼ low

phyllo fruit & nut sheets with spiced milk

SOUPS & SNACKS

sweet corn, leek & lima bean soup

SWEET CORN, LEEK & LIMA BEAN SOUP

1 cup dried lima beans, soaked
   in cold water overnight
2 teaspoons olive oil
1 medium-size leek, sliced
3$\frac{1}{3}$ cups creamed corn
1 cup fresh or frozen corn kernels
5 cups reduced-salt chicken stock
$\frac{1}{3}$ cup basmati rice
2 tablespoons snipped
   fresh chives

1 Rinse the lima beans under cold water. Simmer in a large pan of water for 40 minutes or until soft. Drain and remove any loose skins.

2 Heat the oil in a large pan, add the leek and cook over medium heat for 5 minutes or until soft.

3 Add all the corn, stock and rice. Bring to a boil, reduce heat and simmer, stirring occasionally, for 25 minutes or until the corn and rice are soft.

4 Add the beans and chives to the soup and cook until warmed through. Serve hot. Serves 6

per serving | fat 4.5 g | protein 14.5 g | carbohydrate 52.5 g | fiber 12.5 g | cholesterol 0 mg | energy 310 cal | gi 45 ▼ low

SIMPLE CHICKEN NOODLE SOUP

3$\frac{1}{3}$ oz cellophane noodles
6 cups reduced-salt chicken stock
1 tablespoon reduced-salt
   soy sauce (tamari)
2 medium-size chicken breasts,
   skinless
1 cup sliced snowpeas
3$\frac{1}{3}$ cups broccoli florets
1 cup peas

1 Put noodles into a bowl, cover with boiling water and set aside for 10 minutes or until soft. Drain well.

2 Put the stock and soy into a large frying pan, bring to a boil and reduce heat to a simmer.

3 Add the chicken breasts, cover and cook for 10–15 minutes or until the chicken is tender and its juices run clear when tested with a knife. Remove and allow to cool slightly.

4 Finely shred the chicken and return to the stock.

5 Add the snowpeas, broccoli and peas and cook for 5 minutes or until the vegetables are soft.

6 Divide the noodles evenly among the bowls and ladle soup over the top. Serves 6

per serving | fat 6.5 g | protein 27 g | carbohydrate 19.5 g | fiber 3 g | cholesterol 63 mg | energy 245 cal | gi 39 ▼ low

simple chicken noodle soup

tomato & bocconcini pita pizzas

TOMATO & BOCCONCINI PITA PIZZAS

1 Preheat oven to 425°F.

2 Spread the tomato paste over the pita. Layer the bocconcini and both types of tomato over the paste and drizzle the balsamic evenly.

3 Bake for 10-15 minutes or until the base is crisp and the bocconcini is golden.

4 Scatter the basil leaves over the top before serving. Serves 4 as a snack

per serving | fat 4.5 g | protein 10.5 g | carbohydrate 37 g | fiber 7 g | cholesterol 6.5 mg | energy 235 cal | gi 55 ▼ low

2 tablespoons tomato paste

4 medium-size whole-grain pita bread

2½ oz bocconcini (small, fresh mozzarella cheese), thinly sliced

2 large vine-ripened tomatoes, cut into thick slices

6½ oz cherry tomatoes, halved

2 teaspoons balsamic vinegar

2 tablespoons torn fresh basil leaves

ROAST GARLIC & BEAN DIP WITH PITA CHIPS

1 Preheat oven to 350°F.

2 Put the garlic into a baking dish and bake for 30 minutes or until soft. Remove and discard the skin and set the flesh aside.

3 Cut the pita into triangles, spray lightly with olive oil spray and sprinkle with cumin seeds. Bake on a non-stick baking tray for 15 minutes or until crisp.

4 While the pita chips bake, put the garlic flesh, beans and cream cheese into a food processor and process until creamy. Sprinkle the dip with paprika and serve with pita. Serves 8 as a snack

per serving | fat 6.5 g | protein 6 g | carbohydrate 15 g | fiber 3 g | cholesterol 15.5 mg | energy 140 cal | gi 51 ▼ low

1 head garlic, kept whole and skin on

3 medium-size whole-grain pita bread

olive oil spray

1 tablespoon cumin seeds

13 oz can lima beans, drained weight 10 oz

1 cup light cream cheese

¼ teaspoon paprika

roast garlic & bean dip with pita chips

sweet potato wedges with mint yogurt

SWEET POTATO WEDGES WITH MINT YOGURT

1½ lb peeled orange
  sweet potato
olive oil spray
¼ teaspoon ground cumin
¾ cup non-fat plain yogurt
1 clove garlic, crushed
2 tablespoons finely shredded
  fresh mint

1 Preheat oven to 425°F.

2 Cut the sweet potato into long, thick wedges and lightly spray with olive oil spray. Put onto a non-stick baking tray and bake for 40 minutes or until tender.

3 Put the cumin, yogurt, garlic and mint into a bowl and mix to combine. Serve wedges with yogurt dip on the side. Serves 4 as a snack

per serving | fat 0.7 g | protein 6.4 g | carbohydrate 29.3 g | fiber 3.7 g | cholesterol 2.3 mg | energy 158 cal | gi 47 ▼ low

SWEET CORN WITH SESAME HERB CRUST

4 medium-size cobs sweet corn
1 tablespoon reduced-fat
  polyunsaturated margarine
1 clove garlic, crushed
1 tablespoon chopped
  fresh parsley
2 tablespoons assorted seeds
  (pumpkin, sunflower, sesame)

1 Cook the sweet corn in a large pan of boiling water for 10 minutes or until the kernels are tender. Drain and set aside.

2 Put the margarine, garlic and parsley into a bowl and mix to combine. Spread the mixture evenly down the sides of the corn cobs.

3 Roll the cobs in the seed mix until coated. Serve hot. Serves 4 as a snack

per serving | fat 6 g | protein 4 g | carbohydrate 15.5 g | fiber 3 g | cholesterol 0 mg | energy 130 cal | gi 48 ▼ low

sweet corn with sesame herb crust

ITALIAN VEGETABLE, BEAN & PASTA SOUP

2 teaspoons olive oil

1 medium-size onion,
   coarsely chopped

2 cloves garlic, crushed

1 small eggplant,
   coarsely chopped

2 medium-size red bell peppers,
   seeded and coarsely chopped

1 medium-size green bell pepper,
   seeded and coarsely chopped

2 medium-size zucchini,
   thickly sliced

1 lb 10 oz can chopped tomatoes

1 bay leaf

1 teaspoon dried Italian
   mixed herbs

5 cups reduced-salt
   vegetable stock

13 oz can lima beans,
   drained weight 10 oz

1 cup frozen fava beans,
   defrosted and peeled

3 1/3 oz fettuccine, broken

1 Heat the oil in a large pan, add the onion and cook over medium heat for 5 minutes or until the onion is golden.

2 Add the garlic and eggplant and cook for 5 minutes or until the eggplant is golden.

3 Add the bell peppers and zucchini and cook for 5 minutes or until just tender. Stir in the tomatoes, bay leaf, mixed herbs and stock. Bring to a boil, reduce heat and simmer for 15 minutes or until the vegetables are tender.

4 Add the lima beans, fava beans and fettuccine and cook for 5 minutes, stirring occasionally, or until the fettuccine is al dente (cooked, but still with a bite to it). Serves 6

per serving | **fat 3 g** | **protein 9.5 g** | **carbohydrate 22 g** | **fiber 6.5 g** | **cholesterol 0 mg** | **energy 160 cal** | **gi 38** ▼ **low**

italian vegetable, bean & pasta soup

SWEET POTATO, GINGER & SOYBEAN SOUP

2 teaspoons sesame oil

1 medium-size onion,
   finely chopped

1 tablespoon finely grated
   fresh ginger

3 1/3 cups peeled, chopped orange
   sweet potato

1 tablespoon reduced-salt
   soy sauce (tamari)

5 cups reduced-salt
   vegetable stock

2 star anise

1 cup dried shitake Chinese
   mushrooms, halved

10 oz can soybeans, drained
   weight 7 oz

3 1/3 cups roughly chopped
   broccolini or broccoli

2 tablespoons chopped fresh
   cilantro (coriander)

1 Heat the oil in a large pan, add the onion and ginger and cook over medium heat for 3 minutes or until the onion is golden.

2 Add the sweet potato and cook for 5 minutes or until it starts to soften.

3 Add the soy, stock, star anise, Chinese mushrooms and soybeans. Bring to a boil, reduce heat, cover and simmer for 30 minutes or until the sweet potato is soft.

4 Stir in the broccolini and cilantro, simmer for 3 minutes uncovered or just until the greens wilt. Serve hot. Serves 4

per serving | fat 7 g | protein 14 g | carbohydrate 24.5 g | fiber 6 g | cholesterol 0 mg | energy 215 cal | gi 41 ▼ low

sweet potato, ginger & soybean soup

smoky ham & herb corn bread

SMOKY HAM & HERB CORN BREAD

1 Preheat oven to 350°F. Lightly grease a 9-inch x 3-inch loaf tin or 8 individual serve sized mini loaf tins.
2 Sift the flour, baking powder and paprika into a bowl. Add the cornmeal, cheese, ham, herbs, eggs, soy milk and oil and mix to combine.
3 Spoon the mixture into the prepared tin and decorate with parsley and sunflower seeds.
4 Bake for 45 minutes for the large loaf or 20 minutes for the mini loaves.
5 Allow to cool in the tin for 5 minutes before turning out on a wire rack to cool completely.
6 Serve warm with reduced-fat polyunsaturated margarine. Serves 8 as a snack

per serving | fat 9.5 g | protein 10.5 g | carbohydrate 25.5 g | fiber 1.5 g | cholesterol 56 mg | energy 230 cal | gi 65 ◆ med

* To convert all-purpose flour to self-rising flour, add 2 level teaspoons of baking powder to 1 cup of all-purpose flour.

1 cup self-rising flour*
2 teaspoons baking powder
1 teaspoon sweet paprika
3/4 cup fine cornmeal
1/3 cup grated reduced-fat cheddar cheese
2/3 cup chopped 97% fat-free smoked ham
1/3 cup chopped fresh herbs
2 eggs, lightly beaten
1 cup reduced-fat soy milk
2 tablespoons canola oil
extra fresh parsley leaves, to decorate
2 tablespoons sunflower seeds

DRIED APRICOT & PEACH CEREAL BARS

1 cup dried apricots

1 cup dried peaches

3 cups raw rolled oats

1/3 cup all-purpose flour

2 eggs, lightly beaten

1/4 cup reduced-fat
polyunsaturated margarine

1/2 cup milk cooking
chocolate, chopped

1 Preheat oven to 350°F.

2 Lightly grease and line a 7-inch x 11-inch shallow baking tin.

3 Put the apricots and peaches into a food processor and pulse until finely chopped, or alternatively chop finely with a sharp knife.

4 Put the dried fruit, rolled oats, flour, eggs and melted margarine into a bowl and mix well.

5 Press mixture into the prepared tin and bake for 15–20 minutes or until firm. Cool in the tin.

6 Put the chocolate into a small heatproof bowl over a small pan of gently simmering water. Do not let any water come into contact with the chocolate or it will be ruined.

7 Drizzle the melted chocolate over the slice and allow to set. Use a serrated knife to cut the slice into even bars. Makes 18

per bar | fat 5 g | protein 4 g | carbohydrate 23.5 g | fiber 3 g | cholesterol 21.5 mg | energy 155 cal | gi 40 ▼ low

dried apricot & peach cereal bars

LUNCH

roast beef & horseradish sandwiches

ROAST BEEF & HORSERADISH SANDWICHES

8 slices whole-grain bread

2 tablespoons bottled horseradish

1²/₃ cups thinly sliced lean
  roast beef

³/₄ cup peeled and grated
  fresh beets

1 cup snowpea sprouts

cracked black pepper

1 Spread 4 slices of bread with horseradish.

2 Top with the shaved beef, grated beets and snowpea sprouts. Sprinkle with cracked black pepper. Top with the remaining bread slices, cut and serve. Serves 4

per serving | **fat 6 g** | **protein 23.5 g** | **carbohydrate 33.5 g** | **fiber 4 g** | **cholesterol 44.5 mg** | **energy 285 cal** | **gi 34** ▼ **low**

SUSHI NESTS

1 cup Japanese short-grain rice

1 tablespoon Japanese
  rice vinegar

10 sheets nori seaweed, cut in half

1 small avocado, peeled
  and chopped

20 cooked large shrimp,
  peeled but with tails left on

1 baby cucumber, unpeeled and
  thinly sliced

1 tablespoon pickled ginger,
  finely chopped

wasabi (Japanese horseradish),
  to serve

reduced-salt soy sauce (tamari),
  to serve

1 Put the rice into a pan and add 3 cups cold water. Bring to a boil and cook over medium heat for 5 minutes or until tunnels appear on the surface of the rice.

2 Reduce the heat to low, cover and cook for 10 minutes or until the rice is soft. Remove from heat, stir in the vinegar and set aside to cool.

3 Line 10 x ¹/₃ cup capacity non-stick muffin holes with double thickness nori, spoon 2 tablespoons of rice into each of the holes, then top each equally with avocado, prawns, cucumber and ginger.

4 Lift the nests out gently and serve immediately with wasabi and soy. Makes 10

per nest | **fat 5 g** | **protein 10 g** | **carbohydrate 17 g** | **fiber 3 g** | **cholesterol 57 mg** | **energy 155 cal** | **gi 47** ▼ **low**

sushi nests

smoked trout on pumpernickel bread

SMOKED TROUT ON PUMPERNICKEL BREAD

1 Cut the cucumber and onion into paper-thin slices. Put them into a non-metallic bowl, pour over the vinegar, mix and allow to stand for 10 minutes.
2 Spread the bread with the mayonnaise and top evenly with the sprouts, cucumber and onion.
3 Break trout into large flakes, arrange on top of the cucumber and sprinkle with black pepper. Serves 4
per serving | fat 6.5 g | protein 26.5 g | carbohydrate 49 g | fiber 10 g | cholesterol 55 mg | energy 365 cal | gi 47 ▼ low

2 baby cucumbers, unpeeled
1 medium-size red (Spanish) onion
2 tablespoons apple cider vinegar
8 slices pumpernickel bread
2 tablespoons low-fat mayonnaise
1 cup alfalfa sprouts
1 smoked rainbow trout,
   skin and bones removed
   (10 oz trimmed weight)
cracked black pepper

MEXICAN MEATLOAF

1 Preheat oven to 350°F. Grease and line the base of an 8-inch x 4-inch loaf tin.
2 Put the chicken, cumin, paprika, breadcrumbs, onion, carrot, egg and kidney beans into a bowl and mix to combine.
3 Press the mixture into the prepared tin. Spread the tomato salsa over the top and bake for 45 minutes or until cooked through. Drain off any excess moisture.
4 Serve slices with a leafy green salad. Serves 8
per serving | fat 9 g | protein 30 g | carbohydrate 13.5 g | fiber 3.5 g | cholesterol 119 mg | energy 255 cal | gi 47 ▼ low

2 lb lean ground chicken
1/2 teaspoon ground cumin
1/2 teaspoon paprika
3/4 cup fresh whole-grain
   breadcrumbs
1 medium-size onion, grated
1 medium-size carrot, grated
1 egg, lightly beaten
13 oz can red kidney beans,
   drained weight 10 oz
1/2 cup medium heat, bottled
   tomato salsa

mexican meatloaf

antipasto frittata

ANTIPASTO FRITTATA

3$\frac{1}{3}$ oz fettuccine

2 teaspoons olive oil

1 medium-size onion, thinly sliced

1 cup fresh or frozen fava beans,
   peeled

6 eggs, lightly beaten

$\frac{1}{2}$ cup skim or non-fat milk

2 tablespoons chopped fresh basil

$\frac{1}{3}$ cup grated parmesan cheese

$\frac{2}{3}$ cup canned artichoke hearts
   in brine, drained and quartered

$\frac{2}{3}$ cup semi-dried or sun-dried
   tomatoes

1 Cook the fettuccine in a large pan of rapidly boiling water until al dente (cooked, but still with a bite to it). Drain well and set aside.

2 Heat the oil in a 12-inch non-stick frying pan, add the onion and fava beans and cook over medium heat until the onion is golden.

3 Whisk together the eggs, milk, basil and parmesan and pour into the pan. Arrange the fettuccine, artichokes and tomatoes evenly in the pan. Cook over a low-medium heat for about 10 minutes or until the edges of the egg mixture start to set.

4 Transfer to a preheated broiler and cook under a medium heat for 5–10 minutes or until the center of the egg mixture is just set.

5 Allow to cool for 5 minutes before sliding the frittata out and cutting into wedges. Serve hot or cold with a mixed green salad. Serves 6

per serving | fat 9 g | **protein 15.5 g** | **carbohydrate 20.5 g** | **fiber 5.5 g** | **cholesterol 195.5 mg** | **energy 225 cal** | **gi 35** ▼ **low**

QUICK FRIED RICE

1 tablespoon vegetable oil

4 scallions, sliced

2 eggs, lightly beaten

$\frac{3}{4}$ cup thinly sliced 97%
   fat-free ham

4 cups cooked, cold basmati rice

1 cup fresh or frozen corn kernels

1 cup peas

1 tablespoon reduced-salt
   soy sauce (tamari)

1 Heat the oil in a wok, add the scallions and stir-fry over medium heat for 2 minutes or until soft.

2 Add the eggs and stir gently for 1–2 minutes or just until the eggs begin to scramble.

3 Add the ham and rice and stir fry for 3 minutes. Stir in the corn, peas and soy and heat through. Serve hot or cold. Serves 6

Note: 1$\frac{1}{4}$ cups of uncooked basmati rice yields 4 cups cooked rice.

per serving | fat 6.5 g | **protein 12 g** | **carbohydrate 44 g** | **fiber 3.5 g** | **cholesterol 73.5 mg** | **energy 285 cal** | **gi 56** ◆ **med**

quick fried rice

salmon pasta salad

SALMON PASTA SALAD

1 Cook the pasta in a large pan of rapidly boiling water until al dente (cooked, but still with a bite to it). Rinse under cold water and drain well.
2 Steam the green beans until tender.
3 Break the salmon into large chunks and mix gently together with the pasta, beans, chickpeas, quartered tomatoes, sliced onion, arugula and capers.
4 Whisk together the mustard, vinegar, orange juice and olive oil. Pour the dressing over the salad and mix through. Serves 6

per serving | **fat 8 g** | **protein 22.5 g** | **carbohydrate 45 g** | **fiber 6 g** | **cholesterol 44 mg** | **energy 345 cal** | **gi 42** ▽ **low**

3^1/₃ cups penne pasta
1^2/₃ cups trimmed green beans
14 oz can pink salmon in water
  with no added salt
13 oz can chickpeas (garbanzo
  beans), drained weight 10 oz
8 oz cherry tomatoes
1 medium-size red (Spanish) onion
1 cup arugula
2 tablespoons chopped capers
3 teaspoons whole-grain mustard
2 tablespoons balsamic vinegar
¼ cup unsweetened orange juice
1 tablespoon olive oil

THAI CHICKEN & GREEN HERB SALAD

1 Put noodles into a bowl, cover with boiling water and set aside for 10 minutes or until soft. Drain well.
2 Put the chicken breasts into a deep frying pan, cover with water and simmer over low heat for 20 minutes or until tender. Allow to cool slightly, then remove from the liquid and shred finely.
3 Cook the beans and snowpeas in boiling water for 2-3 minutes or until bright green and just tender. Drain and rinse in cold water.
4 Put the noodles, chicken, beans, snowpeas, scallions, cucumber, cabbage and mint into a bowl and toss to combine.
5 Whisk together the lime juice, apple juice, oyster sauce and sesame oil and pour over the salad. Toss together and serve. Serves 6

per serving | **fat 6 g** | **protein 22.5 g** | **carbohydrate 19 g** | **fiber 2 g** | **cholesterol 63 mg** | **energy 225 cal** | **gi 38** ▽ **low**

3^1/₃ oz cellophane noodles
2 medium-size lean chicken
  breasts, trimmed of skin and
  any visible fat
1^2/₃ cups trimmed green beans
1 cup thinly sliced snowpeas
3 scallions, chopped
1 baby cucumber, thinly sliced
2 cups Chinese cabbage,
  finely shredded
1 cup fresh mint leaves
3 tablespoons lime juice
¼ cup unsweetened apple juice
1 tablespoon oyster sauce
1 teaspoon sesame oil

thai chicken & green herb salad

macaroni & cheese with ham & spinach

MACARONI & CHEESE WITH HAM & SPINACH

1⅓ cups macaroni

2 tablespoons reduced-fat
   polyunsaturated margarine

¾ cup finely sliced 97%
   fat-free ham

1½ tablespoons all-purpose flour

1¾ cups skim or non-fat milk

1 teaspoon whole-grain mustard

1 cup baby spinach,
   roughly chopped

⅓ cup grated reduced-fat
   cheddar cheese

sea salt

cracked black pepper

1 Cook the pasta in a large pan of rapidly boiling water until al dente (cooked, but still with a bite to it). Drain well and keep warm.

2 Heat the margarine in a frying pan, add the ham and cook over medium-high heat for about 5 minutes or until browned.

3 Stir in the flour and cook, stirring continuously, for 1 minute. Remove the pan from the heat and gradually whisk in the milk. Return to the heat and cook, stirring constantly, for about 2 minutes or until the sauce boils and thickens.

4 Stir in the mustard, spinach and cheese and season to taste with sea salt and pepper. Cook just until the cheese melts.

5 Add the pasta to the pan and stir to coat the pasta with the sauce. Serve immediately. Serves 4

per serving | **fat 8 g** | **protein 19.5 g** | **carbohydrate 43 g** | **fiber 2 g** | **cholesterol 25 mg** | **energy 320 cal** | **gi 46** ▼ **low**

GRILLED VEGETABLE & RICOTTA SALAD

10 oz peeled, sliced orange
   sweet potato

2 medium-size red bell peppers,
   cut into thick strips

2 medium-size zucchini

6½ oz portobello mushrooms

1 cup no-oil, no-sugar plain
   salad dressing

8 slices whole-grain bread

2 cups baby spinach

½ cup reduced-fat ricotta
   cheese, crumbled

⅓ cup sunflower seeds

1 Put the sweet potato, bell peppers, zucchini and mushooms into a bowl and pour over all but 2 tablespoons of salad dressing. Mix thoroughly.

2 Remove the crusts from the bread and brush the slices with remaining dressing.

3 Cook the vegetables and bread on both sides in a preheated ridged sauté pan until the vegetables are tender and the bread is grilled.

4 Put the vegetables, bread, spinach, ricotta and sunflower seeds into a bowl and toss gently to combine. Serve hot or cold. Serves 4

per serving | **fat 10.2 g** | **protein 16.3 g** | **carbohydrate 40.7 g** | **fiber 8.7 g** | **cholesterol 13 mg** | **energy 341 cal** | **gi 44** ▼ **low**

grilled vegetable & ricotta salad

DINNER

oven-baked fish with chips & tartare

OVEN-BAKED FISH WITH CHIPS & TARTARE

2 tablespoons finely grated
   parmesan cheese
3/4 cup dry breadcrumbs
1 tablespoon chopped fresh dill
8 (2 1/2 lb) trimmed, firm white
   fish fillets
1 egg white, lightly beaten
1 lb unpeeled baby potatoes,
   cut into thick wedges
olive oil spray
2 tablespoons capers, chopped
3 small gherkins, chopped
2 scallions, trimmed and chopped
3 tablespoons low-fat mayonnaise
3 tablespoons low-fat
   plain yogurt
lemon wedges, to serve

1 Preheat oven to 425°F.
2 Put the parmesan, breadcrumbs and dill onto a flat plate and mix to combine. Dip the fish into the egg white and coat in the crumb mixture.
3 Put the potatoes into a baking dish, spray lightly with olive oil spray and bake for 20 minutes or until the potatoes are golden and tender.
4 Arrange the fish on a separate non-stick baking tray, spray lightly with the olive oil spray and put into the oven with the potatoes for the last 10 minutes of baking. The cooked fish will flake apart easily when tested with the tip of a knife.
5 To make the tartare sauce, put the capers, gherkins, scallions, mayonnaise and yogurt into a bowl and mix to combine. Serve the fish and chips with tartare sauce and wedges of lemon. Serves 6
per serving | fat 4.5 g | protein 32.5 g | carbohydrate 24.5 g | fiber 2.5 g | cholesterol 77 mg | energy 270 cal | gi 52 ▼ low

CHINESE PORK, SOY & SNOWPEAS

2 teaspoons vegetable oil
1 lb lean ground pork
1 clove garlic, crushed
4 scallions, sliced
6 1/2 oz can water chestnuts,
   drained weight 4 1/2 oz
10 oz can soybeans, drained
   weight 7 oz
2 cups sliced snowpeas
2 tablespoons oyster sauce
8 iceberg lettuce leaves

1 Heat the oil in a wok, add the pork and stir-fry over medium heat for 5 minutes, or until browned.
2 Add the garlic and scallions and cook for 2 minutes more or until the scallions soften.
3 Add the water chestnuts, soybeans, snowpeas and oyster sauce and simmer for 10 minutes.
4 Serve bowls of the pork mixture accompanied by the lettuce leaves and allow each person to roll up their own leaves with the pork. Serves 4
per serving | fat 14.5 g | protein 32.5 g | carbohydrate 10.5 g | fiber 5.5 g | cholesterol 75 mg | energy 300 cal | gi 24 ▼ low

chinese pork, soy & snowpeas

soba noodles with seafood & snowpeas

SOBA NOODLES WITH SEAFOOD & SNOWPEAS

1 Cook the soba noodles in a medium-size pan of cold water until they come to the boil, add another cup of water and stir until they return to a boil. Cook for 5 minutes or until tender. Drain well.

2 Heat the oil in a wok, add the garlic, ginger and onion and stir-fry over medium heat for 3 minutes or until the onion is soft.

3 Add the seafood and stir-fry over high heat for 3 minutes. Add the soy, honey, stock, lemon, snowpeas and broccolini or broccoli and stir-fry for 3 minutes, or until the vegetables are just tender.

4 Serve nests of the noodles with the seafood mixture mounded on top. Serves 4

per serving | fat 4.5 g | protein 48.5 g | carbohydrate 64.5 g | fiber 10 g | cholesterol 267 mg | energy 475 cal | gi 46 ▼ low

10 oz dried soba (buckwheat) noodles
2 teaspoons olive oil
2 cloves garlic, crushed
1 tablespoon grated fresh ginger
1 medium-size onion, thinly sliced
1½ lb mixed, cleaned seafood seafood (large shrimp, calamari, mussels, scallops)
1 tablespoon reduced-salt soy sauce (tamari)
2 teaspoons honey
½ cup reduced-salt fish stock
2 teaspoons grated lemon zest
2 cups snowpeas
3⅓ cups chopped broccolini or broccoli

TOFU, VEGETABLE & RICE NOODLE STIR-FRY

1 Rinse the noodles under cold water to separate.

2 Heat the oils in a wok, add the ginger and tofu and stir-fry over high heat for 3 minutes or until the tofu is golden.

3 Add the carrot, corn and bell pepper and stir-fry for 3 minutes or until the vegetables are soft.

4 Add the bok choy, soy, stock and noodles and stir-fry for 3 minutes or until heated through.

5 Remove from heat and toss through the bean sprouts. Serve hot. Serves 4

per serving | fat 13.5 g | protein 20 g | carbohydrate 60 g | fiber 6.5 g | cholesterol 0 mg | energy 440 cal | gi 35 ▼ low

1 lb fresh rice noodles
1 teaspoon sesame oil
1 tablespoon vegetable oil
1 tablespoon grated fresh ginger
2 cups cubed firm tofu
1 carrot, peeled and sliced
3⅓ oz baby corn, halved
1 medium-size red bell pepper, seeded and sliced
1 bunch baby bok choy, leaves separated
2 tablespoons reduced-salt soy sauce (tamari)
½ cup reduced-salt vegetable stock
1 cup bean sprouts

tofu, vegetable & rice noodle stir-fry

fettuccine with roast tomato & peppers

FETTUCCINE WITH ROAST TOMATO & PEPPERS

6¹/₂ oz cherry tomatoes

6 plum tomatoes

1 head garlic, separated into
   cloves but not peeled

1 medium-size red bell pepper,
   seeded and cut into thin strips

olive oil spray

13 oz fettuccine

¹/₂ cup fresh basil

13 oz can borlotti beans, drained
   weight 10 oz

2 cups baby arugula

¹/₂ cup grated parmesan cheese,
   to serve

1 Preheat oven to 400°F.

2 Halve the cherry and plum tomatoes and put with garlic and bell pepper into a large baking dish. Spray lightly with olive oil spray and season with pepper.

3 Bake for 40 minutes or until the plum tomatoes are soft. Peel the garlic and discard the skins.

4 Cook the pasta in a large pan of rapidly boiling water until al dente (cooked, but still with a bite to it). Drain well and return to the pan.

5 Add the roasted vegetables. Stir in the basil leaves, beans, arugula and parmesan and toss gently to combine. Serves 4

per serving | fat 4.5 g | protein 16.5 g | carbohydrate 62.5 g | fiber 7 g | cholesterol 6.5 mg | energy 350 cal | gi 40 ▼ low

GRILLED LAMB WITH WARM TABBOULEH

1¹/₂ cups reduced-salt chicken stock

1 cup bulghur wheat

8 oz cherry tomatoes, halved

1 cup chopped fresh
   flat-leaf parsley

¹/₂ cup chopped fresh mint

4 scallions, sliced

1 tablespoon extra virgin olive oil

2 tablespoons lemon juice

1 lb lean lamb loin

¹/₂ teaspoon ground allspice

8 vine leaves preserved in brine

olive oil spray

1 cup low-fat hummus

6 whole-grain pita bread

1 Put the stock into a pan and bring to a boil. Add bulghur wheat, reduce heat, cover and simmer for 15 minutes or until liquid is absorbed. Remove from the heat and set aside uncovered for 10 minutes.

2 Stir through the tomatoes, parsley, chopped mint, scallions, olive oil and lemon and keep warm.

3 Rub the lamb with the allspice and wrap in the vine leaves. Cook in a lightly olive oil-sprayed, preheated ridged sauté pan for 3−5 minutes on each side, or until cooked to your liking.

4 Rest the lamb in a warm place for 5−10 minutes before slicing. Serve with warm tabbouleh, hummus and pita bread. Serves 6

per serving | fat 9.5 g | protein 27 g | carbohydrate 37.3 g | fiber 9.4 g | cholesterol 54 mg | energy 359 cal | gi 46 ▼ low

grilled lamb with warm tabbouleh

CHICKEN TAGINE WITH SPICED CHICKPEAS

2 teaspoons olive oil

8 skinless medium-size chicken drumsticks

1 medium-size onion, sliced

¼ teaspoon saffron threads

11 oz peeled orange sweet potato, cut into chunks

2 medium-size zucchini, cut into thick slices

1 tablespoon finely shredded orange zest

½ cup dried apricots

½ cup dried pitted prunes

13 oz can chopped tomatoes

2 cups reduced-salt chicken stock

1 cinnamon stick

6½ oz pearl barley

13 oz can chickpeas, (garbanzo beans), drained weight 10 oz

2 tablespoons roughly chopped, fresh flat-leaf parsley

1 Heat the oil in a large heatproof casserole dish or Dutch oven, add the chicken in batches and cook over medium heat for 3–5 minutes or until browned.

2 Return all the chicken to the pan, add the onion and saffron and cook for 5 minutes or until the onion is soft and translucent.

3 Add the sweet potato, zucchini, orange zest, dried fruit, tomatoes, stock and cinnamon stick. Bring to a boil, reduce heat, cover and simmer gently for 40 minutes.

4 Remove the lid and cook for 10 minutes or until the chicken comes away from the bone.

5 While the chicken is cooking, put the barley into a pan, cover with 4 cups water and bring to a boil. Simmer, uncovered, for 25 minutes.

6 Add the chickpeas to the barley and cook for 5 minutes more, or until both are tender. Drain well, then stir in the parsley. Serve mounds of the barley mixture topped with the tagine. Serves 8

per serving | **fat 8.5 g** | **protein 24 g** | **carbohydrate 41.5 g** | **fiber 8 g** | **cholesterol 88.5 mg** | **energy 335 cal** | **gi 33** ▼ **low**

chicken tagine with spiced chickpeas

LEMON HERB TUNA WITH RICE & LENTILS

1 cup brown lentils, soaked in
   cold water overnight
1 tablespoon olive oil
4 medium-size onions, thinly sliced
1/4 cup reduced-salt chicken stock
1 cup basmati rice
4 (1 1/4 lb) trimmed tuna steaks
olive oil spray
1/2 cup chopped fresh
   flat-leaf parsley
1/2 cup chopped fresh cilantro
   (coriander)
3 cloves garlic, crushed
1 teaspoon ground cumin
1 teaspoon paprika
juice and zest of 1 lemon
2 tablespoons fat-free dressing

1 Drain and rinse the lentils and discard any small stones. Put in a medium-size pan and just cover with water. Bring to a boil, reduce heat and simmer for 10 minutes, then drain well.

2 Heat the oil in a large, deep frying pan, add the onion and cook over medium heat for 5 minutes or until soft. Add the stock and cook for 10 minutes more,
or until the stock evaporates and the onions brown.

3 Add the rice, lentils and 3 cups water, bring to a boil and simmer for 5 minutes or until tunnels appear on the surface. Cover with foil, reduce the heat to low and cook for 10–15 minutes more or until the rice is soft.

4 Cook the tuna in a lightly olive oil-sprayed, preheated ridged sauté pan for 2–3 minutes on each side, or according to your preference.

5 Put the parsley, cilantro, garlic, spices, lemon juice, zest and dressing into a bowl and whisk to combine. Serve the tuna sprinkled with herb sauce and rice to the side. Serves 4

per serving | fat 14.5 g | protein 57 g | carbohydrate 65 g | fiber 10 g | cholesterol 57 mg | energy 620 cal | gi 45 ▼ low

lemon herb tuna with rice & lentils

beef, bean & mushroom burritos

BEEF, BEAN & MUSHROOM BURRITOS

1 Heat the oil in a large frying pan, add the onion and cook over medium heat for 3 minutes or until the onion is soft.

2 Add the beef and cook for 5 minutes until browned. Add the bell peppers and mushrooms and cook for about 5 minutes or until soft.

3 Add the beans, tomatoes and corn, bring to a boil and simmer for 15 minutes or until sauce has thickened slightly. Stir in the cilantro.

4 Spread some of the meat mixture down the center of a tortilla and roll up to enclose filling.

5 Arrange the rolled tortillas in a large ovenproof dish. Spoon the salsa evenly over the top and sprinkle with grated cheese.

6 Bake for 20 minutes or until the cheese is golden. Serve with a mixed green salad. Serves 6

per serving | fat 10.5 g | protein 25.5 g | carbohydrate 45.5 g | fiber 9.5 g | cholesterol 32.5 mg | energy 380 cal | gi 36 ▼ low

2 teaspoons olive oil

1 medium-size onion, chopped

12 oz lean ground beef

1 red bell pepper, seeded and chopped

1 green bell pepper, seeded and chopped

10 oz mushrooms, sliced

13 oz can ready-made chilli beans

13 oz can chopped tomatoes

1 cup fresh or frozen corn kernels

2 tablespoons chopped fresh cilantro (coriander)

8 flour tortillas, 8 inches in diameter

1½ cups mild bottled tomato salsa

¼ cup grated reduced-fat cheddar cheese

LAMB SHANKS, MUSHY PEAS & GRAVY

1 tablespoon olive oil

4 (1 lb 1⅓ oz trimmed weight)
   Frenched lamb shanks

8 pickling onions, peeled
   and left whole

2 cloves garlic, crushed

2 cups reduced-salt beef stock

½ cup red wine

1 bay leaf

4 black peppercorns

6½ oz peeled baby carrots

3⅔ cups frozen peas

4 teaspoons reduced-fat
   polyunsaturated margarine

1 Heat the oil in a large heatproof casserole dish or Dutch oven. Add the lamb shanks in batches and cook over medium heat until browned all over. Return all the lamb to the pan.

2 Add the onions and cook for 3–5 minutes or until browned, then add the garlic and stir. Add the stock, red wine, bay leaf and peppercorns. Cover and simmer gently for 45 minutes.

3 Add whole carrots and cook for 15 minutes more, or until carrots are tender and the lamb comes away from the bone. Remove the lamb, carrots and onions, cover and keep warm.

4 Increase the heat, boil liquid for 10 minutes or until reduced and thickened slightly.

5 Put the peas into a pan, cover with water, bring to a boil and simmer for 10 minutes or until tender. Drain well and add the margarine, then roughly mash together with the peas.

6 Serve the lamb shanks and vegetables with a mound of mashed peas and sprinkle the sauce over the top. Serves 4

per serving | **fat 9.5 g** | **protein 40.5 g** | **carbohydrate 18.5 g** | **fiber 9.5 g** | **cholesterol 84 mg** | **energy 345 cal** | **gi 38** ▼ **low**

lamb shanks, mushy peas & gravy

SWEET THINGS

baked mango & passionfruit custards

BAKED MANGO & PASSIONFRUIT CUSTARDS

½ cup thinly sliced mango flesh

1 cup reduced-fat milk

3 eggs, lightly beaten

¼ cup sugar or low-calorie
  sweetener suitable for cooking

½ cup passionfruit pulp or
  orange juice

1 Preheat oven to 350°F.

2 Arrange the mango in 4 x ½ cup capacity ramekins.

3 Whisk together the milk, eggs, sugar or sweetener and passionfruit or juice and pour over the mango.

4 Bake the custards for 20 minutes or until they are just set. Serve warm. Serves 4

per serving (sugar) | fat 5 g | protein 8.5 g | carbohydrate 23 g | fiber 5 g | cholesterol 145 mg | energy 170 cal | gi 56 ◆ med

per serving (sweetener) | fat 5 g | protein 8.5 g | carbohydrate 11.5 g | fiber 5 g | cholesterol 145 mg | energy 125 cal | gi 37 ▼ low

SEMOLINA CAKE WITH VANILLA PEARS

1 cup self-rising flour*

1½ cups semolina

⅓ cup sugar or low-calorie
  sweetener suitable for cooking

2 teaspoons finely grated
  lemon zest

3 eggs, lightly beaten

¾ cup non-fat, sugar-free
  vanilla yogurt

¼ cup reduced-fat
  polyunsaturated margarine

4 medium-size pears, unpeeled,
  uncored and sliced lengthwise

1½ cups unsweetened apple juice

1 vanilla bean, halved lengthwise

1⅔ cups non-fat, sugar-free
  vanilla yogurt, to serve

1 Preheat oven to 350°F. Lightly grease and line an 8-inch spring form tin.

2 Sift the flour and semolina into a bowl and stir in sugar or sweetener and zest. Whisk together the eggs, yogurt and melted margarine and mix into the dry ingredients until smooth. Pour into the tin.

3 Bake for 40–50 minutes or until a skewer comes out clean when inserted into the center. Cool in the tin for 5 minutes then turn out on a wire rack.

4 Put the pears, apple juice and vanilla bean into a pan and bring to the boil. Reduce heat, cover and simmer for 10 minutes or until the pears are just soft. Serve the pears with cake and yogurt. Serves 10

per serving (sugar) | fat 5.8 g | protein 9.5 g | carbohydrate 49.2 g | fiber 2.8 g | cholesterol 61 mg | energy 291 cal | gi 50 ▼ low

per serving (sweetener) | fat 5.8 g | protein 9.5 g | carbohydrate 42 g | fiber 2.8 g | cholesterol 61 mg | energy 263 cal | gi 48 ▼ low

* To convert all-purpose flour to self-rising flour, add 2 teaspoons baking powder to 1 cup all-purpose flour.

semolina cake with vanilla pears

apple & grape jell-o

APPLE & GRAPE JELL-O

1 Put the gelatin or jell-o and apple juice into a pan and stir over low heat for 2 minutes or until the gelatin dissolves. Remove from the heat and cool slightly.
2 Divide $1/3$ cup of the fruit among 4 x 1 cup capacity glasses.
3 Pour in enough of the apple liquid to cover the fruit, cover and chill the glasses for 20 minutes or until just set.
4 Divide the remaining berries and grapes among the glasses, pour over the remaining liquid and chill for 4 hours or until set. Serves 4

per serving | **fat 0 g** | **protein 4 g** | **carbohydrate 32.5 g**
| **fiber 1 g** | **cholesterol 0 mg** | **energy 140 cal**
| **gi 41** ▼ **low**

4 teaspoons gelatin or jell-o
3 cups unsweetened apple juice
$2/3$ cup strawberries, cut
   into halves
$12/3$ cups seedless green
   or black grapes

PEACH & GRAPEFRUIT GRANITA WITH CITRUS

1 Put the sugar or sweetener, grapefruit juice, sliced peaches and juice into a pan. Stir over low heat until the sugar dissolves.
2 Pour into a shallow non-reactive metal container. Freeze until the mixture starts to harden around the edges, then break up the crystals with a fork.
3 Return to the freezer for 1 hour, break up with a fork, repeat the whole process and freeze again.
4 Put the segmented oranges, grapefruit, tangerines and orange flower water into a non-metallic bowl and mix to combine.
5 Serve the granita in chilled glasses with citrus salad to the side. Serves 6

per serving (sugar) | **fat 0.5 g** | **protein 2.5 g**
| **carbohydrate 30 g** | **fiber 3 g** | **cholesterol 0 mg**
| **energy 140 cal** | **gi 44** ▼ **low**
per serving (sweetener) | **fat 0.5 g** | **protein 2.5 g**
| **carbohydrate 25 g** | **fiber 3 g** | **cholesterol 0 mg**
| **energy 120 cal** | **gi 38** ▼ **low**

2 tablespoons sugar or low-calorie
   sweetener suitable for cooking
3 cups pink grapefruit juice,
   unsweetened
13 oz can peaches in juice
2 medium-size navel oranges,
   cut into segments
3 pink grapefruit, segmented
2 tangerines, segmented
1 teaspoon orange flower water

peach & grapefruit granita with citrus

rhubarb & mixed berry ricotta sponge

RHUBARB & MIXED BERRY RICOTTA SPONGE

2 cups chopped rhubarb

¼ cup unsweetened apple juice

2 tablespoons sugar or low-calorie sweetener suitable for cooking

1⅓ cups fresh or frozen mixed berries

6½ oz prepared plain sponge cake

½ cup low-fat ricotta cheese

¾ cup non-fat, sugar-free vanilla yogurt

1 Preheat oven to 350°F.

2 Put the rhubarb in a pan with the apple juice and sugar or sweetener and stir over low heat until the sugar dissolves.

3 Cover and cook for 5 minutes, then add the berries, cover and cook for another 5 minutes or until the rhubarb is soft.

4 Cut the sponge cake into 8 even slices. Put the ricotta and yogurt into a bowl and mix to combine.

5 Arrange 2 sponge slices on each plate and top with the ricotta mixture and stewed fruit. Serves 4

per serving (sugar) | fat 5.2 g | protein 11.5 g | carbohydrate 47.6 g | fiber 3.2 g | cholesterol 93 mg | energy 281 cal | gi 47 ▼ low

per serving (sweetener) | fat 5.2 g | protein 11.5 g | carbohydrate 40.1 g | fiber 3.2 g | cholesterol 93 mg | energy 253 cal | gi 41 ▼ low

LOW-FAT ICE CREAM CASSATA SLICE

10 oz low-fat chocolate ice cream, softened

⅓ cup pine nuts, roughly chopped

8 oz low-fat vanilla ice cream, softened

½ cup dried apricots, roughly chopped

⅔ cup dried figs, chopped

½ cup dried peaches, roughly chopped

¼ cup red and green glacé cherries, chopped

1 Line an 8-inch x 4-inch bar tin with enough plastic wrap to hang down the sides of the tin.

2 Put the chocolate ice cream and pine nuts into a bowl and mix to combine. Spoon the mixture into the base and up the sides of the tin, leaving the center hollow. Freeze until firm.

3 Mix the vanilla ice cream with the dried fruit and spoon into the bar tin over the chocolate ice cream. Smooth the surface and cover with overhanging plastic wrap. Freeze overnight or until firm.

5 Remove from the tin, discard the plastic and slice with a knife heated under hot water. Serves 6

per serving | fat 6.5 g | protein 5.5 g | carbohydrate 35 g | fiber 4.5 g | cholesterol 7 mg | energy 220 cal | gi 44 ▼ low

low-fat ice cream cassata slice

banana, pear & pistachio nut bread

BANANA, PEAR & PISTACHIO NUT BREAD

1 Preheat oven to 350°F. Grease and line an 8-inch
x 4-inch loaf tin.
2 Put the pears into a bowl and just cover with
boiling water for 10 minutes or until soft. Drain well.
3 Sift the flours, baking powder and cinnamon into
a bowl. Stir in the sugar or sweetener and nuts.
4 Whisk together the eggs, buttermilk and oil and stir
through the dry ingredients, banana and pears.
5 Spoon the mixture into the prepared tin and bake
for 55–60 minutes or until a skewer comes out clean
when inserted into the center. Cool in the tin for
5 minutes, then turn out on a wire rack. Serves 10

per serving (sugar) | fat 8 g | protein 7.5 g
| carbohydrate 47.5 g | fiber 4.5 g | cholesterol 40 mg
| energy 290 cal | gi 55 ▼ low

per serving (sweetener) | fat 8 g | protein 7.5 g
| carbohydrate 44.5 g | fiber 4.5 g | cholesterol 40 mg
| energy 280 cal | gi 54 ▼ low

* To convert all-purpose flour to self-rising flour, add
2 teaspoons baking powder to 1 cup all-purpose flour.

1 cup dried pears, roughly chopped
2¼ cups self-rising flour*
½ cup plus 1 tablespoon
    all-purpose flour
1 teaspoon baking powder
1 teaspoon ground cinnamon
3 tablespoons brown sugar
    or low-calorie sweetener
    suitable for cooking
⅓ cup pistachio nuts, chopped
2 eggs, lightly beaten
1 cup buttermilk
2 tablespoons vegetable oil
1 cup mashed ripe banana

POACHED SAFFRON FRUIT POTS WITH PHYLLO

1 Preheat oven to 400°F.
2 Put the fruit, saffron, cinnamon, orange juice, zest
and apple juice into a pan. Bring to a boil, reduce
heat, cover and simmer for 10 minutes or until the
fruit is soft. Spoon into 6 x 1 cup capacity ramekins.
3 Brush each of the phyllo sheets with melted
margarine, cut into 6 equal squares and scrunch
into 24 balls. Arrange on top of the fruit.
4 Bake for 10 minutes or until the pastry is crisp
and golden. Serve immediately. Serves 6

per serving | fat 2 g | protein 4 g | carbohydrate 62 g
| fiber 10.5 g | cholesterol 0 mg | energy 275 cal
| gi 38 ▼ low

1 cup dried apricots
1 cup dried pears
⅔ cup dried figs
½ cup dried pitted prunes
pinch saffron threads
1 cinnamon stick
juice and zest of 1 orange
1 cup unsweetened apple juice
4 sheets phyllo pastry
2 teaspoons reduced-fat
    polyunsaturated margarine

poached saffron fruit pots with phyllo

baked cherry rice custard

BAKED CHERRY RICE CUSTARD

3 tablespoons basmati rice

2 cups water

3 eggs, lightly beaten

2 tablespoons sugar

1 teaspoon vanilla

2¹/₂ cups skim or non-fat milk

13 oz can pitted cherries,
  drained weight 9 oz

1 Preheat oven to 350°F.

2 Put the rice and water into a pan, boil uncovered for 10 minutes then drain well. Whisk together the eggs, sugar, vanilla and milk. Add rice and mix.

3 Pour into a 4 cup capacity ovenproof dish and scatter cherries over the top.

4 Put the dish into a deep baking tray. Pour hot water into the tray until it is halfway up the dish sides. Bake for 50 minutes or until set. Serves 6

per serving | fat 2.5 g | protein 8 g | carbohydrate 25.5 g | fiber 1 g | cholesterol 97 mg | energy 160 cal | gi 45 ▼ low

QUICK-MIX FRUIT CAKE

2 cups mixed dried fruit

2 cups golden raisins

1 cup dried apricots, chopped

²/₃ cup blanched almonds, chopped

¹/₂ cup reduced-fat
  polyunsaturated margarine

¹/₂ cup brown sugar or low-calorie
  sweetener suitable for cooking

1¹/₂ cups unsweetened apple juice

³/₄ cup stone-ground
  all-purpose flour

1 cup self-rising flour*

2 teaspoons mixed spice
  (optional)

2 eggs, lightly beaten

2 cups low-fat custard

1 Preheat oven to 315°F. Grease and line an 8-inch round cake tin with 2 layers of baking paper.

2 Put the fruit, almonds, margarine, sugar or sweetener and apple juice into a pan and simmer for 2 minutes. Transfer to a bowl and cool.

3 Sift flours and spice into a bowl, add eggs and fruit and mix to combine. Spoon into the tin and smooth the top with wet fingers. Wrap several layers of newspaper around the tin and secure with kitchen string.

5 Bake the cake for 1¹/₂–2 hours or until a skewer comes out clean when inserted into the center. Cool briefly in the tin, then turn out on a wire rack. Serve warm with custard or cold. Makes 16 slices

per serving (sugar) | fat 8.9 g | protein 5.9 g | carbohydrate 59.3 g | fiber 4 g | cholesterol 25.4 mg | energy 341 cal | gi 49 ▼ low

per serving (sweetener) | fat 8.9 g | protein 5.9 g | carbohydrate 53.1 g | fiber 4 g | cholesterol 25.4 mg | energy 318 cal | gi 47 ▼ low

* To convert all-purpose flour to self-rising flour, add 2 teaspoons baking powder to 1 cup all-purpose flour.

quick-mix fruit cake

antioxidant - a substance that prevents body tissues from being damaged by oxidation caused by free radicals, which are thought to be associated with many disease processes and are formed in the body naturally or from exposure to pollution, cigarette smoking, chemicals and the sun.

carbohydrates - a group of nutrients that includes starches, sugars and fibers. All carbohydrates, except for fibers, are made up of sugar units. They are broken down into sugars during digestion. Different carbohydrates are made up of chains of sugars bound together in different ways. They are both digested and their sugar absorbed into the blood at different rates (see glycemic index on pages 6-7).

glucose - a type of sugar that makes up the starches and some sugars found in foods. Starches are broken down into glucose during digestion, which is then absorbed into the bloodstream and becomes blood glucose (blood sugar), the main fuel for the brain and muscles.

hypoglycemia - the term for a lower than normal blood glucose level, often called a 'hypo'. It can be due to taking too much insulin or diabetes medication; not eating enough carbohydrate or missing a meal; drinking alcohol without food; or stress or extra exercise. Symptoms include feeling cold and weak, sweating, shakiness, irritability, confusion, and dizziness, and if blood sugar continues to fall it can lead to unconsciousness and coma.

insulin - a hormone secreted by the pancreas in response to rising blood sugar, which enables body cells to take up glucose from the blood, causing the blood glucose level to drop back down to normal. It also stimulates cells to take up fats and proteins from the blood.

omega-3 essential fats - polyunsaturated fats that have to be obtained from the diet because they cannot be made in the body. They are found in walnuts, linseed, canola oil, and oily fish like tuna, salmon, trout and mackerel. Increasing the intake of omega-3 fats while reducing saturated fat intake can help improve insulin action, reduce blood pressure and promote good circulation.

sweeteners and sugar substitutes - these can be either: 1. Nutritive sweeteners, which contain calories and increase blood sugar (eg, sugar, corn syrup, fructose, glucose, honey, maltose, fruit juice concentrate); 2. Sugar alcohols, which contain fewer calories and have a lower blood sugar response (eg, sorbitol, mannitol, isomalt); or 3. Non-nutritive or low-calorie sweeteners which are far sweeter than sugar and used in tiny amounts, so they provide almost no calories and won't increase blood sugar (eg, aspartame, acesulfame-K, Splenda®). Many 'lite' or reduced-sugar versions of sweet foods, such as soft drinks and jam, contain sugar alcohols and/or low-calorie sweeteners and can usually be consumed in moderation by people with diabetes.

Recipes & styling Jody Vassallo
Photographer Ben Dearnley
Home economist Angela Treggoning
Recipe tester Camilla Jessop
Props stylist Melissa Singer
Designer Nicole Vonwiller
Editor Lynelle Scott-Aitken
Consulting nutritionist Dr Susanna Holt

DISCLAIMER: The nutritional information listed under each recipe does not include the nutrient content of garnishes or any accompaniments not listed in specific quantities in the ingredient list. The nutritional information for each recipe is an estimate only, and may vary depending on the brand of ingredients used, and due to natural biological variations in the composition of natural foods such as meat, fish, fruit and vegetables. The nutritional information was calculated by a qualified dietitian using FoodWorks dietary analysis software (Version 3, Xyris Software Pty Ltd, Highgate Hill, Queensland, Australia) based on food composition tables and food manufacturers' data. Where not specified, ingredients are always analysed as average or medium, not small or large. All recipes were analysed using 59 g eggs.

IMPORTANT: Those who might be at risk from the effects of salmonella food poisoning (the elderly, pregnant women, young children and those suffering from immune deficiency diseases) should consult their general practitioner about consuming raw or undercooked eggs.

THE DIABETES EVERYDAY COOKBOOK
Published by
Marlowe & Company
An Imprint of Avalon Publishing Group Incorporated
245 West 17th Street · 11th Floor
New York, NY 10011-5300

Library of Congress Cataloging-in-Publication Data

Vassallo, Jody.
    The diabetes everyday cookbook / Jody Vassallo, with Susanna Holt.
    p. cm.
    ISBN 1-56924-426-X
    1. Diabetes—Diet therapy—Recipes. I. Holt, Susanna.
    II. Title
    RC662.V37 2004
    641.5'6314—dc22

                                    2003066603

9 8 7 6 5 4 3 2 1

Printed in Canada
Distributed by Publishers Group West